Mildred Lewis Rutherford
"Miss Millie"

THE CIVILIZATION OF THE OLD SOUTH
What Made It, What Destroyed It, What Has Replaced It

by
Mildred Lewis Rutherford
Athens, Georgia
Past Historian General of the
United Daughters of the Confederacy

With an Appendix by
Miss Winnie Davis
"The Daughter of the Confederacy"

THE CONFEDERATE REPRINT COMPANY
☆   ☆   ☆   ☆

WWW.CONFEDERATEREPRINT.COM

The Civilization of the Old South:
What Made It, What Destroyed It,
and What Has Replaced It
by Mildred Lewis Rutherford

Originally Published in 1916
The MacGregor Company
Athens, Georgia

Reprint Edition © 2016
The Confederate Reprint Company
Post Office Box 2027
Toccoa, Georgia 30577
www.confederatereprint.com

Cover and Interior Design by
Magnolia Graphic Design
www.magnoliagraphicdesign.com

ISBN-13: 978-1945848063
ISBN-10: 1945848065

CHAPTER ONE

☆ ☆ ☆ ☆

The Civilization of the Old South[1]

The civilization of the Old South was truly unique – nothing like it before or since, nor will there ever be anything like it again.

Henry R. Jackson said:

"The stern glory of Sparta, the rich beauty of Athens, the splendors of Imperial Rome, the brilliancy of ancient Carthage – all pale before the glories of the Old South, the South as our forefathers lived it, the South as Washington, Jefferson, and Madison lived it, and, last but not least, the South as our Robert E. Lee lived it."

And Henry Grady said:

"In the honor held above estate; in the hos-

---

1. The following text was delivered orally to a meeting of the United Daughters of the Confederacy at the Municipal Hall in Dallas, Texas on 9 November 1916.

5

pitality that neither condescended nor cringed; in frankness and heartiness and wholesale comradeship; in the reverence paid to womanhood and the inviolable respect in which woman's name was ever held the civilization of the Old South has never been surpassed, and perhaps will never again be equalled by any people or nation upon this globe."

It is true that it has been compared to the Feudal System of the Middle Ages, when military lords exercised jurisdiction over serfs, allotted them land, collected taxes from them and in return demanded service in time of war – but there was no love lost between lord and serf.

It has been compared to the English tenant system, where the landlord leases the land, and, so long as the rent is paid, all is well, but if the tenant fails to pay his rent, then be is ejected without mercy – very rarely is there any love lost between the landlord and his tenant.

Very different was the relation that existed between the slave-holder and his slaves under the institution of slavery as it was in the Old South. By the way, the negroes in the South were never called slaves – that term came in with the Abolition crusade. They were our servants, part of our very home, and always alluded to as the servants of a given plantation or town home – as, "the servants of White Marsh," "the servants of Warner Hall," "the servants of Rosewall or Rosewell," or of Halseot "the servants of Cherry Hill," "the servants of Round Hill, of Silver Hall," etc. The servants had no surnames of their own before the war – they had none when they came to us from Africa – but they were known by the names of their owners or owners' estates. Thus it was that Nancy from the Thornton plantation after freedom became Nancy Thornton; and Tom from Warner Hall became Tom Warner.

There was something in the economic system of the Old South that forged bonds of personal interest and affection between the master's family and their servants – a pride that was taken the one in the other. The master would boast, "My servants are the best on all the plantations round, best workers, best mannered, most contented, the healthiest." And the servants in turn would say, "Our white folks are quality folks they're none of your po' white trash. Aint nobody in the world like our 'ole Marster' and 'ole Mis'."

The negroes under the institution of slavery were well-fed, well-clothed and well-housed. A selfish interest, if no nobler or higher motive, would have necessitated this, for the slave was the master's salable property. He would not willingly have allowed him to be injured physically.

How hard it was for us to make the North understand this!

I never heard of a case of consumption, or rather tuberculosis among the negroes before the War between the States, and now negroes are dying by the hundreds yearly. I never heard of but one crazy negro before the war. Now asylums can not be built fast enough to contain those who lose their minds.

Negroes were immune from yellow fever before the war, and now this is no longer true.

I never saw a drunken negro before the war, for they were not allowed to buy, sell or drink liquor without the master's consent, and crimes now so prevalent, largely on account of drunkenness, were unheard of then.

The negroes were forced to go to church and white pastors employed to preach to them. They were not allowed to work on Sunday. In proportion to population, there were more negroes as church members than whites.

Marriage licenses must be obtained and the marriage take place in the presence of "Ole Marster" or the overseer.

Under the institution of slavery, the negro race increased more rapidly than the white. The reverse is the case today.

The servants were very happy in their life

upon the old plantations. William Makepeace Thackeray, on a lecture tour in America, visited a Southern plantation. In "The Roundabout Papers" he gives this impression of the slaves:

"How they sang! How they danced! How they laughed! How they shouted! How they bowed and scraped and complimented! So free, so happy! I saw them dressed on Sunday in their Sunday best – far better dressed than our English tenants of the working class are in their holiday attire. To me, it is the dearest institution I have ever seen and these slaves seem far better off than any tenants I have seen under any other tenantry system."

When a white child was born a negro of corresponding age was given. This negro owned the white child as much as the white child owned the negro. The negro refused to take an order from any young person save the owner and the owner refused to have any order given by any one but the owner. Close ties of affection grew between the two. As an illustration of this, in a child's game "Playing Dead," my sister was allowed to be covered in the leaves as dead but my Ann Eliza could not play dead.

How restful the old life was! What a picture of contentment, peace and happiness it presented! It was something like our grandmothers' garden as compared with the gardens of today.

The old-fashioned gardens with box-bordered beds so dignified and orderly and stately, with four o 'clocks, holly hocks, larkspurs, touch-me-nots, wall flowers, bachelor buttons, snap dragons, migonette, sweet alyssum, columbine and sunflower. How beautiful they were! What lovely overdresses the four o 'clocks made for our flower dolls! What beautiful wreaths the larkspurs made, purple and white, which we pressed without compunction in the finest books in our father's library, totally unconscious of the ugly stain left behind.

There were long walks bordered with cape jessamine, banana shrubs, Chinese magnolias, crepe myrtle, rose beds filled with moss roses, (I never see a pink moss rose now,) yellow roses, red and pink single roses, tube roses; fences covered with Cherokee roses; summer houses covered with honeysuckle, yellow jasmine, woodbine, wisteria or white clematis. The odor of sweet grass and mimosa blooms, the rows of flowering pomegranate bushes, with double blossoms and the bearing pomegranate with single blossom – apple trees in which the mocking birds' nests were found, and no one white or black could rob a mocking bird's nest, and, in the spring, doves cooing to their mates – that's like the old-time days never to return again.

The plantation was the center of social life in the old system and the "Big House" was the center of plantation life. It was always full and room for more. When all the beds were filled, pallets were made on the floors all over the house, and this gave trouble to no one for there were plenty of servants to do the bidding, and mattresses, feather beds, pillows, quilts, blankets and marvelous counterpanes in profusion, and linen closets always full.

In the "Big House" there lived "Ole Marster" and "Ole Mis'." There were "Young Marster" and "Young Mis'," and the children. Then there were the uncles and aunts and cousins to remotest kinship, with carriages, wagons, horses and servants. This gave trouble to no one, for there was plenty in the corn crib, plenty in the barn, plenty in the smokehouse, plenty in the pantry, plenty of turkeys, geese, ducks, guineas, chickens and squabs. Plenty of eggs, plenty of butter, cheese, cream, curds, clabber, sweetmilk and buttermilk – barn full, yard full, dairy full, pantry full. Shelves lined with jellies, jams, apple butter, quince and peach preserves, brandy peaches, marmalade, and large stone jars filled with pickles, sweet and sour.

The table fairly groaned with good things

to eat, and there were no cooks like grandmother's old cooks. The kitchen was never in the house but way out in the yard. This mattered little then, for there were plenty of little negroes to run back and forth with the covered dishes and hot batter cakes, hot waffles, hot rolls and even hot ginger cakes. You young people will say, "But it was not stylish to have so much on the table." No, not stylish, but far better than the little "dabs of nothingness" that you have today.

You may say, "What sinful waste!" Yes, there was a waste but it was not sinful, for white and black had enough and to spare. The household servants always had what the white people at the Big House had, and the poor whites near by, if any, had more from Ole Mis' generous hand.

The stables were full of riding horses, buggy horses, carriage horses and ponies, so riding parties were the amusement for mornings and afternoons. Every girl and boy in the Old South learned to ride and drive at an early age. The little boys helped to take the horses to water, and to break the wildest colts. This made the masters' sons the finest cavalrymen in the Confederate Army.

In the evenings, old Uncle Ned, the fiddler, would come into the great wide hall and the Virginia Reel would be danced, Ole Marster leading off with the prettiest girl there as his partner. Then the dignified minuet would be called for, and Ole Marster would lead out Ole Mis' with the gallantry of Sir Gallahad and wind up with the cotillion, old Ned calling out the figures, keeping time with his foot and head, as he would sing out, "Salute your pardners," "Swing your pardners," "Sachez to the right," then "Sachez to the left," and finally, "Promenade all."

Young people, we could not have danced the "Turkey Trot" nor the "Bunny Hug" had we desired.

Early hours were kept on the old plantation, for every one must be stirring at daybreak. Ole Mis' would be the first to rise. Hers was a busy life. She started all the household servants to their work – the dry rubbers, and brass polishers. Ah, how those brass fenders, andirons and candlesticks shone! They had few carpets in those days and so the floors had to be polished by being dry rubbed. The garments had to be cut out for the seamstresses, and the looms gotten ready for the weavers, and the spinning wheels had to be started, breakfast had to be given out and the cooks must begin their work.

Early in the morning, you could hear the beating of the dough – no biscuit mills then – and if we had beaten biscuits, they were made with "elbow grease." You could hear the milkers as they went down to the cow lot, calling the little negroes to keep off the calves. You could hear Aunt Nanny feeding the chickens, with her "chick, *chick,* CHICKEE," with a rising intonation of the voice on the last "chickee," and then a cackle, and we knew one of the chickens for breakfast was about to meet its fate and have its neck wrung. No refrigerator in those days to keep the chickens on ice over-night.

I can see Ole Mis' now with her basket of medicines on her arm going from cabin to cabin doctoring the sick babies and the old negroes. Frequently all night long she lingered at the bed-side of some dying negro, praying with him and when life had ceased, would close the staring glassy eyes. None in the "Big House" knew of this nightly vigil save "Ole Master."

I can hear the musical ring of the bunch of keys fastened to her side, or in her key basket, as she walked along, for, while Uncle Eben kept the crib key, and Aunt Lishy the dairy key, and Aunt Nanny the smokehouse key, Ole Mis' always kept the pantry key. She gave out every meal herself, weighed the flour, sugar, butter, lard and meal, measured the coffee, and she always skimmed the cream in the dairy and prepared the milk for the churns, and made the curds.

There was such an unjust article to the South in *The New York Times* last year (1915). Edna Ferber, the authoress, is represented as saying that "The kitchens of the Southern women were left to the device of a company of slaves who ran the house pretty much to suit themselves. The Southern women never knew what provisions there were in the kitchen or cellar or how much food went out each day to furnish feasts in the near-by cabins. They knew nothing of housekeeping."

What absolute ignorance this showed of life in the Old South! Fortunately a Southern girl who had statistics in hand was ready to answer Miss Ferber. She found in a trunk of papers and letters belonging to her great grandmother who lived on her plantation in Washington Co., Ga., facts to contradict this in a most certain way. She found the "Plantation Book of 1851," in which the daily routine of work by the mistress of the plantation was given. In this memorandum book was kept not only the household duties, but how many lbs. of cotton had been picked by the women and children on the plantation – "Martha 806 lbs., Mary 1,243 lbs., and Eliza 920 lbs." etc., and the prize money allowed them for picking over a certain amount, and then "something to George who couldn't pick, but who helped with the baskets."

Then followed the exact weight of the lard and the meat given to each family –"John and his family 62 lbs. of meat, Lewis, Patty and Martha 30 lbs." Then the amounts given to the decrepit negroes in the cabins. Finally the prescriptions left by the doctor for two of her negro patients. Then the death of a negro baby is recorded. The birth and death of the negroes were always recorded in the Family Bible at the Big House.

Now when Miss Sarah Prince Thomas (Carol North) sent her answer to the article in *The New York Times*, and asked that it be printed to contradict Miss Ferber's statements, it was returned, saying that they did not need it. Was this just?

From early childhood we of the South were taught all work was honorable, and every act, even sweeping a room or picking up chips could be made as acceptable in God's sight as any service an archangel could perform.

Each child had some special duty every day. The girl, as soon as she was able to hold a needle or know upon what finger to put the thimble, was made to hem the towels, the table napkins, the tablecloths, the servants aprons, or to aid in drying the cut glass and silver, for Ole Mis' always looked after this herself; and the boys were given the care of some one animal to feed and care for, or some gates to lock and unlock, and no one else, not even the negro each child owned, was allowed to do this work for them.

It is true the aristocrat of the Old South did not go into his blacksmith shop to shoe his horse, nor his wife into the kitchen to cook, or to the wash tub to wash, but it was not because they were ashamed or scorned to do it, but because there was no need for them to do these things.

History has greatly maligned the old aristocrat of the South. He was not "haughty," he was not "purse proud," and he did not consider himself "of finer clay" than any one else, as history has unjustly represented him.

Aristocracy then was guaged by manners and morals and not by the size of the bank account, as I fear is too much the case today. Far more time was spent in cultivating the graces and charms of life than in amassing fortunes. They realized that "Manners are of more importance than money and laws" – far manners give form and color to our lives. They felt, as Tennyson said, "Manners are the fruit of lofty natures and noble minds."

It will take us a long time to undo the falsehoods of history about the civilization of the Old South.

Who was the head of the plantation? Why, Ole Mis'; everyone on the plantation must obey Ole Mis'; and Ole Marster said so and he obeyed Ole Mis' too. Her life was a long life of devotion – devotion to her God, devotion to her church – she was really the pillar of the church – devotion to her husband, to her children, to her kinfolks, to her neighbors and friends and to her servants. She could not be idle for she must ever be busy.

Ole Marster could delegate many of his duties to the overseer, while he entertained his guests. He would rise early in the morning, eat his breakfast – and such a breakfast! Broiled chicken, stuffed sausage, spareribs, broiled ham and eggs, egg bread, corn muffins, hot rolls, beaten biscuits, batter cakes or waffles with melted butter, syrup or honey and the half not told. I can taste those waffles now. My, how delicious they were! Then, after smoking his Havana cigar, he would mount his saddle horse and ride over the plantation to see if the orders given the day before had been fully carried out. Then he would give the next day's orders, ride to a neighboring plantation, and return in time for an early dinner. Dinner was always at midday on the old plantation. If it were summer time, Ole Marster would lie down upon the wide veranda or in the spacious hall upon one of those old mahogany sofas covered with black horse hair and a little darkey with a turkey tail fan or a peacock feather brush standing at his head to fan him and keep off flies, while he took his noon-day nap. If it were winter, he would go into his library and, before a large, open fireplace with whole logs of wood, he would discourse upon the topics of the day with visitors.

There was no subject with which Ole Marster was not at home – whether politics, philosophy, religion, literature, poetry or art. Ole Marster's sons for generations had been well educated and had a perfect familiarity with the classics – they could read Greek and Latin better than some of us can read English today. The best magazines of the day were upon his library table, and the latest books upon his library shelves.

There were no public schools in the South before the Reconstruction period. The teachers on the plantations were tutors and governesses from the best colleges of the North and South, and in the private schools in the towns and cities were men and women whose education was beyond question. It was somewhat different in the Old Field Schools. There the teacher sometimes knew little beyond "readin'" and "'ritin'" and "'rithmetic,'" and was considered very learned if he carried his scholars beyond "the rule of three."

Ole Marster was rarely as religious as Ole Mis' and, if he wouldn't have family prayers, Ole Mis' would, but Ole Marster always had a reverence for religion and made his negroes attend church regularly and raised his children with a reverence for Sunday and holy things.

Ole Mis' often put on a grandmother's cap when only thirty-five – what will the young grandmother of today say to that? Girls married at an early age, for a home was ready –"They never came out for they had never been in."

How handsome Ole Marster was in his broadcloth suit and his silk beaver hat, his pump-soled boots, his high stock and collar, and his gold watch and chain with fob. Bill Arp said the aristocrat was known by the way he toyed with the fob upon his chain.

How quaint and beautiful Ole Mis' was in her lace cap and satin bows! I wish I had a black silk apron with pockets in it like my grandmother used to wear. What long deep pockets there used to be in the skirts – sometimes pockets on both sides!

The entertainments would last for weeks at neighboring plantations ten or twenty miles apart. The old family carriage would come before the door, and the maids with the band boxes and the valets with the horse-hair trunks, with brass nail heads, would strap them behind and cover them with a leather curtain, then they would follow the young people in a spring wagon to the place of entertainment. I can see now just such a party the old family carriage, high up on elliptical springs, the driver's seat above the top of the carriage, and the steps which unfolded down, and then folded up.

The footman was there to let down the steps, the lovers were there to assist in mounting the steps, and Bill Arp said the true aristocrat was known not only by the size of her foot but by the graceful way she could manage her crinoline in mounting the steps of the carriage or descending therefrom. The lovers would mount their horses and act as a body-guard to the appointed place.

The girls were dressed in dainty lawns and muslins – for no girl before her marriage, or until she had passed the marriageable age, was allowed to wear velvet, silk, satin or lace. On their heads were the daintiest straw bonnets trimmed with pink roses – a bunch over each ear – and bows of pink ribbons to tie beneath the chin, and the dearest black net gloves and the daintiest black slippers with low heels, or no heels at all. Their lovers would have thrown not only their cloaks, Sir Walter-like, but themselves in the mud rather than those dainty feet should be soiled by the mud. And it was considered *dreadful if more than the tip of that slipper should show.* What would our grandmothers' have said to these short dresses of today?

Hunting parties, riding parties, fishing parties, boating parties, tournaments, charades, dances, and all sorts of joys never dreamed of by the young people of today – no sitting out in the moonlight on the lawns, no hiding in dark corners of the verandas, no love-making after the old people had gone to bed, no automobile rides after dark, no dancing until daylight, and consequently runaway marriages were rarely heard of – and divorces were rarer. While the young men were on their fox hunts, the young girls would be employed with their embroidery – exquisite work they did!

But, oh, the preparation for a wedding feast! Weeks beforehand the plans were laid. "Hunter's round" had to be packed in spices, fruit cake to be made, raisins seeded, citron sliced, almond blanched, and later the cakes iced, pyramids of cakes graduating in octagon shape from very large at the bottom to small at top and capped with a figure of the bride with her wedding veil and the groom in black broadcloth that had been bought from some confectionery shop.

Little fence rails of icing around the different layers of cakes mounted one upon the other; bunches of grapes made of icing and covered with gold or silver leaf; roses made of white tarlatan and rimmed with icing. How we used to stand around – white children and black – and beg for the cones or the bowls that held the icing after the cakes were finished! I can see, now, the little smeared faces – for the owners unhesitatingly licked the bowls. Then the blanc mange shaped in so many wonderful molds of pineapple, muskmelon, rabbits and roses. Then pig's feet jelly, so stiff, and cut into little squares just big enough for a mouthful – how delicious they were!

Then the day of the wedding! There was the making of the chicken salad and the slicing of the beef tongue and ham and the roasting of turkeys and the icing of the little cakes, the making of the wafers that fairly melted in the mouth, and then the sweet wafers rolled over and oh! so crisp and delicious, and beaten biscuit by the bushel, the watermelon rind preserves cut into such exquisite shapes, fish and bird and flower, and shaded with an artist's eye – the pride of the housekeeper, brought out to be seen if not to be eaten – the mango pickles, peach pickles, brandy peaches, artichoke pickles, cucumber pickles and cherry pickles! Then the boiled custard and the syllabub – we had no ice cream in those days for manufactured ice was unknown.

Every member of the family present had to take home some of the wedding cake, every young person must have some of the cake to dream on, and to name the corners of the room.

The wedding guests lingered on for days and even weeks after the wedding was over, and the feasting continued until the last guest was gone.

Those happy days are no more – gone, never to return, and the civilization as our grandmothers' lived it went with it. Happy are those whose memory holds these days in remembrance! My heartfelt sympathy goes out to those who shall never know of them!

Veterans, didn't we have a good time when hog killing time came! Weren't the pig tails and the crackling bread fine? Don't we feel sorry for these young people who never ate a roasted pig tail, or never spent a Christmas on the old plantation?

Time was measured to Christmas, and three weeks before Christmas Day the wagons would go to the nearest city or town to lay in the Christmas supplies. Every negro man had to have a complete outfit from hat to shoes; every negro woman had to have the same, from head handkerchief to shoes; each negro child every article of clothing needed; and warm shawls, and soft shoes, or some special gifts had to be bought for the old negroes too feeble to work. Then there were the barrels of apples, oranges, cocoanuts, boxes of almonds, Brazilnuts, English walnuts, hazelnuts, raisins, citron and currants; then candies galore, kisses with adorable verses, sugar plums, lemon drops, gum drops, peppermint, cinnamon and lemon candy by the quantity, and last but not least, some mysterious packages that were stowed in mother's large wardrobe, which mammy told us with a grave shake of the head were *"Laroes catch medloes,"* and for fear they might be animals that would bite us, we religiously let them alone, and forget to ask about them when Christmas was over.

How happy all were, white and black, as the cry of "Christmas Gif'" rang from one end to the other of the plantation, begin-fling early in the morning at the Big House and reaching every negro cabin – Christmas can never be the same again.

As in family life when a child is disobedient and must be punished, so in plantation life a disobedient or unruly negro had to be whipped or punished. It was natural that he should prefer to run away to escape a punishment he justly deserved and knew he would surely receive, especially tempted to run into a free State when incentives were offered to him to come and be transported by some underground way and hidden from the owner. It was perfectly natural also for him to give the most exaggerated reports of his treatment to willing listeners who really set a premium upon these exaggerations.

"Aunt Cinthy," living in Florida where Northern tourists so often go for the winter, understood this. When reproached for saying what was absolutely false about the condition of the negro under slavery, she said: "Honey, I am jest obleeged to zaggerate a leetle about these things to edify the Northern tourists – they wouldn't give me any money if I didn't."

The unnatural thing to the Southern planter was how educated and intelligent men and women of the North could believe he would willingly injure his salable property, by hitching him to a plow, or allowing him to be cruelly beaten. To him there was no difference between hiding his negro worth $1,200, or more, and hiding his pocket book which contained the same amount of money. This interference with his personal property was stealing no matter how viewed and it irritated him beyond measure. He knew perfectly well, should he retaliate by taking the horses of these abolitionists from their stables, or cows from their barns, or cattle from their fields, or furniture from their homes, or bank notes from their pockets, it would quickly have been a question of law and imprisonment.

It has been estimated that 75,000 negroes were thus hidden from their owners before 1860.

These fanatics took out "Personal Liberty Bills" contrary to the Constitution, to protect them on the plea that there was a Higher Power than the Constitution. Indeed, in their fanaticism, they publicly burned the Constitution and even said, if the Bible stood for slavery, better burn the Bible, too.

Now, there is no doubt that this was one of the many interferences with Southern rights which forced Southern men to advocate secession in order to secure the rights guaranteed to them by the Constitution. Many think because this interference with the runaway slaves was one of the *occasions* of war that the war was fought to hold the slaves. Never was there a greater mistake. Out of the 600,000 men in the Confederate army 400,000 never owned slaves. What were those men fighting for? There were 315,000 slave-holders in the Northern army. Did they wish their slaves freed? Gen. Lee freed his slaves before the war began. Gen. Grant did not free his until the XIII Amendment passed, for Missouri's slaves were not intended to be freed by the Emancipation Proclamation.[2]

Southern men always believed in State Sovereignty, and Southern men always have stood by the Constitution. Fair-minded Northern men saw this and said the South had by the Constitution the right to secede and contended that the Abolition Party was only a minority party in the North. George Lunt of Boston said, "The majority of the men in the North felt outraged at the actions of the Republican party at the time in interfering with the rights of the Southern States."

Had the South prevailed, the Union would have been preserved and that too by the Constitution. Our negroes would have long ago been freed by gradual emancipation, as Southern slaveholders had already done, were desirous of doing still, and, had no interference come from the abolitionists, there would be now no race problems to adjust.

Neither would there have been any need to change the Constitution except to legislate more strongly to enforce the laws against the

---

2. It was actually Grant's wife, Julia, who owned four house-servants throughout the war. Grant himself freed his one slave before the war in 1859.

slave trade as it was being still carried on by Northern States contrary to law, and the right to free their own slaves, as was claimed by the slaveholders of the Southern States. State Sovereignty would still remain, while the inexpediency of secession would have been proven by war. We would have, today, not only a grander and more glorious Union with no danger threatening us from a centralized government, but we would have a true democracy with State Rights stressed, as President Wilson advocates, a government formed *of* the people, *by* the people and *for* the people knowing no North, no South, no East, no West.

CHAPTER TWO

☆　☆　☆　☆

What Made the Civilization
of the Old South

It was, undoubtedly, the institution of slavery.

Why then did not the institution of slavery as it existed in Egypt, in Greece, in Rome, in Russia, in France, in the British Colonies, in New England and other Northern States produce the same civilization? That it did not, history has proven. There must have been another reason, then, than the mere institution itself.

The difference evidently was in the slave-holders of the South – men of that old Cavalier stock having the fear of God which gave them minds tuned to justice, and hearts trained to love, and pocketbooks opened to the needs of humanity, and I think the open pocketbooks had much

31

to do with it. These men of the Old South lived with open-handed hospitality. One rarely heard of slaveholders in the South amassing great wealth like Stephen Girard of Philadelphia, or Peter Faneuil of Boston, Mass. The Southern slaveholders did not drive close bargains but were generous in all their dealings, believing in the doctrine of "live and let live." Many slaveholders lived far beyond their means, and the surrender found them greatly in debt on account of liberality to their slaves.

From Jamestown and Plymouth Rock flowed two mighty streams of influence – dissimilar and, for more than a hundred years, entirely separate – two types of men with distinct ideals of life. One loved England and the established church, and came simply to investigate the New World and its possibilities, and fully intended to return to England some day and had no desire to withdraw from the mother church.

The other had no love for England and had a grievance against the established church, deliberately planned to make a new home in this country, and never desired or intended to return to the mother land or mother church.

The backbone of the Virginia stream, or the Jamestown Colony, was composed of men from leading families in England, gentlemen of the best English society, the landed gentry born to wealth and very loyal to their king. They were of the Cavalier stock. Many had lost their fortunes by high living, no doubt, and desired to come to this new world, expecting to find it a veritable Eldorado. When they decided to remain, they patterned their social institutions after England, where they had been accustomed to large landed estates with tenants or servants. Coming with this old patriarchal idea of life, they became an agricultural people, making a diffusive civilization, settling on burgesses or plantations, having their indentured servants and living as in their old home.

Not so with the New England stream or Plymouth Rock Colony. They, too, were Englishmen, but did not come from the landed gentry, but from Puritan stock. They had a grievance with England in regard to an interference with their liberty to worship God as they pleased. They did not love the king or the landed gentry, so they began to lay the foundations of new social institutions and to set up new altars of justice and religion, and thus really became autocrats in the administration of the law.

The Jamestown Colony coming from English blood born to rule, their very instincts of life tended to develop political leaders and statesmen.

Their life on the plantations under the institution of slavery in controlling their slaves, fitted them to control themselves and others, so we find for fifty out of seventy years of the early government of our Republic, Southern men filled the Presidential chair. Every man from the South was re-elected for a second term and two offered a third term, while not a President from other sections during this period ever held a second term. Thus was the ability of Southern men to control the affairs of State acknowledged by the people of the country.

The Plymouth Rock Colony, settling in towns and cities, made a cohesive civilization and developed traders, manufacturers, and men fitted for commercial control of the country. Their nearness to each other in the cities and towns also developed literary instincts, and there the leading men of letters were found during those early days of the Republic. A literary atmosphere was created by close contact and Massachusetts particularly produced many poets and philosophers, and the finest essay writers of that day came from New England.

These people were a methodical, painstaking people, exact in all business calculations, in all State regulations. They instigated research, and undertook historical investigations and so we find not only the statistics regarding their affairs accurately kept, but everything pertaining to their history recorded.

The Jamestown Colony did not write their history or accurately keep their statistics – hence we are suffering for this today, because our statistics have been prepared by those who did not know them as we did not know them ourselves, and we are often forced to go to the British Museum and other archives in England to find some of the history of those early days.

While the men of the South were eminently literary, they could not as in New England create a literary atmosphere, for they lived miles apart and rarely had any opportunity to meet in groups to discuss literary topics. They had the ability to write books, and they wrote much for local papers, but there was no need to print books for the money that would come to them from the printing.

The South produced great orators, and great political statesmen whose writings have come down in the political history of our country, excelled by no other section.

The Jamestown Colony thought little of the value of statistics. They were big-hearted, open-handed, free livers, given to hospitality, and as was said before, often lived far beyond their means. The care of their slaves was always a very heavy expense. The institution of slavery brought on an immunity from drudgery and gave leisure for the cultivation of the mind and manners. It made gentlemen and gentlewomen. There was little attempt at grandeur or display – a beautiful simplicity was the charm of the life of the Old South. There was no need to study ethics, it was inborn in white and black. While there were different degrees of wealth – one man owning more slaves than another, or men of business affairs in the towns and cities owning few or no slaves, yet there was little difference in social standing – the line being drawn on education, manners and morals more than on the family tree and the pocketbook. Intellectual advantages and manners were to them of paramount importance. Character always counted for more than blood or money. And sneer as one may at the chivalry of the Old South, it was that which sweetened Southern life. Southern men were not only the champions of the women of their own households, but the protectors of all women.

Now, while the Plymouth Rock Colony also produced gentlemen and gentlewomen, they were of a different type. While at heart they may have been just as true, they lacked the social graces, and charming manners that the civilization of the Old South produced.

This difference came out very strikingly when Thomas Jefferson and John Adams were at the same time representatives from the United States Government in France. They had with them their daughters, Martha Jefferson and Abigail Adams – both well educated young women. Queen Marie Antoinette said that Martha Jefferson had the most exquisitely gracious manners she had ever seen in any young girl, and could be at home in any royal court; while the prim manners of Abigail Adams, the little New England maid, oppressed her.

The Jamestown settlers and their descendants, while not Puritanical in their religion, were religious. While Jonathan Edwards was preaching "hell torments" from a New England pulpit, the churchmen in Virginia were preaching "The love of God to sinful dying men."

Read that tablet on Old Cape Henry Lighthouse commemorating the planting of the Crass by thirty members of that Jamestown Colony, April 26, 1607.

Read Richard Crashaw's Prayer, that was used in the daily service at Jamestown, in which is found:

"Arm us against difficulties, and strengthen us against base thoughts and temptations. Give us faith, wisdom and constancy in thy service."

Read how the Rev. Robert Hunt held daily services under the stretched sails of one of those first three vessels that brought over this first permanent English Colony.

Go to Jamestown Island today and see the remains of that old church built there. Read the history of that church and see in Virginia churches today the remains of the communion service used there.

Read of that *first* Fast Day, and that *first* Thanksgiving Day before even the Pilgrim Fathers had left England.

Read of the missionary work of Alexander Whitaker, the *first* Protestant missionary to American Indians.

Yes, they were religious, but they believed in a religion of joy and happiness and never believed in a religion that carried a long and sanctimonious face.

The Plymouth Rock Colony were Puritans in word and deed. They recognized no church, no creed, no king by divine right. They said they were only responsible to God and to their own consciences. Life with them was simply a preparation for death, but their liberty became intolerance, and having been persecuted they also began to persecute. They allowed no Christmas festivities, no May Day joys, and their children were actually punished for being merry. A man was even forbidden to kiss his wife on Sunday. Nathaniel Hawthorne once said, "Let us thank God for such ancestors, but let us also thank Him that each generation brings us one step farther on in the march of ages."

The Cavaliers and their descendants and the men who settled the Southern colonies, into whose blood came that of the Irish, the Scotch, the Welsh, the French Huguenots, made up a people who have no superiors in the world – and today, after all these years, the purest Anglo Saxon blood out of rural England is to be found in the Southern States, and Englishmen have testified that the purest English is spoken not in New England but in the Southern States.

The Puritans and their descendants and the other colonies that settled the North, into whose blood came the Dutch, the Swedes, the Danes, the Quakers, made a sturdy race, whose strength of character and business qualifications have always made them prominent as men of large affairs in the business world, and has given them great prominence in religious activities and ability in financing large undertakings.

While it is written that Robert Morris, of Pennsylvania, financed the Revolution, we must not forget that Thomas Nelson, of Virginia, borrowed, on his own credit, $2,000,000 for the Continental Congress and this money was never returned to him.

By the way, it was the American Revolution that brought the Cavalier and Puritan with their descendants close together to form one deep, swift current of national life, and the difference in Puritan and Cavalier blood was forgotten in the one mighty united effort to gain American independence.

When Massachusetts suffered, every Southern colony suffered with her and quickly came to aid her. George Mason, of Virginia, wrote to his children to go in deep mourning when the services were held to pray for the relief of Massachusetts. When the Boston Port Bill passed, every one of the Southern colonies responded with aid to Massachusetts.

At the time of the Revolution, every colony was a slave-holding colony. There really was no question of abolition of slavery and no sectional feeling until the time of the Missouri Compromise in 1820, which drew attention to the political power of the slave-holding States.

How did African slavery enter the Southern Colonies?

I wish every one of you would read Mrs.

Sophie Lea's "Synoptical Review of Slavery" She was State Historian of Kentucky, U.D.C. and gives sonic fine statistics of the institution of slavery. Read also Prof. Bingham's articles regarding slavery, and Cobb's *Law of Slavery*, and what Thomas Nelson Page says in his *Old South*.

Who was most responsible for the bringing over of African slaves – the North or the South?

How glad I am to right a wrong against Massachusetts! It was a Dutch vessel, in 1619, sailing the English flag that sold to the Jamestown Colony the first twenty "NEGARS," as John Rolfe called them. This was one year before the *Mayflower* set sail from England, so Massachusetts cannot be blamed for that. That they were sold and not indentured is proven beyond doubt from authorities incontrovertible – such authority as George Bancroft, (Vol. 1, p. 125) America's greatest historian; and Lyon Gardiner Tyler, Virginia's authority on Colonial history.

The strongest testimony is a paper in the possession of the descendants of Gov. Yeardley, who was one of the Jamestown Colony to buy these Africans. He says they were bought in a spirit of humanity with no thought of later commercial value. These creatures were suffering horribly on that slave ship and the Jamestown settlers felt they must be relieved, so bought them, and then tried to civilize them by putting them to work.

If African slavery was a sin, the Spaniards and English were the sinners. It is true the slave trade in the United States was begun by Massachusetts, and in the main carried on by her, not as a private enterprise, but by the authority of the Plymouth Rock Colony. (*Colonial Entry Book*, Vol. IV., p. 724.)

The statute of establishing perpetual slavery was adopted by Massachusetts, Dec., 1641. (*Mass. Historical Coll.,* Vol. VIII., p. 231.)

The slave ship *Desire* sailed from Marblehead, Mass., and was the first to sail from any English colony in America to capture Africans.

The first State to legislate in favor of the slave trade was Massachusetts.

The first State to urge a fugitive slave law was Massachusetts. (Moore's *History of Slavery*.)

The last State to legislate against the slave trade was Massachusetts.

The last slave ship to sail from the United States was the *Nightingale* from Massachusetts in 1861. She secured a cargo of 900 Africans, and was captured by the *Saratoga* under Captain Guthrie, April 21, 1861, after Fort Sumter had been fired on. There is no record that any punishment followed this violation of this law.

The slave trade did not cease with the abolition of slavery in New England and did not cease when the U. S. made it contrary to law in 1807. (Weeden's *History*, Vol. II., p. 835.)

Massachusetts sold, but never freed her slaves.

Augustus Hemmenway, of Boston, died in 1870, leaving to his children in his will, slaves then living in Cuba.

Between 1859 and 1860, 85 slave ships from New York brought over annually thirty to sixty thousand Africans who were sold to Brazil – no record is given of punishment by law that followed. (*Cyclopedia of Political Economy*, Vol. III., p. 733.)

During those same years 75 slave ships sailed from other Northern ports.

"The Cradle of Liberty" in Boston, Faneuil Hall, was built by Peter Faneuil, its owner, from slave trade money.

Girard College, in Philadelphia, was built by Stephen Girard with money made by African slaves on a Louisiana plantation.

The *Wanderer* was sent to Georgia in 1858 and 1859 by the New York Yacht Club with a cargo of slaves. It landed first at Savannah and then at Brunswick, and the slaves were sold.

Henry R. Jackson, a lawyer of Savannah,

tried to convict all Georgians for buying these slaves or having any part in violating the law but failed to find proof to convict.

The *Clotilde* sailed from Mobile, Ala., to win a wager made by Capt. Timothy Meaher of Maine, her owner, that the law could be violated in the South and African slaves could be landed and sold on Southern soil and not be punished. The cargo did sail from Mobile, returned and landed, but the slaves were not allowed to be sold, the scheme thus proving to the owner of the vessel a great financial loss.

Slavery was abolished in the Northern Colonies from no conscientious scruples, but simply because the slave labor was unprofitable. (Fiske's *Critical Period of American History*, p. 73.)

There were five slave markets in the United States, not one built by Southern slaveholders: One in Boston, 1712; one in New York, 1711; one near Cincinnati, Ohio; one in St. Augustine by Spaniards; one in New Orleans by Spaniards. (See T. R. R. Cobb, *Law of Slavery*) There is a slave market photographed in Louisville, Ga., and so marked, but the oldest citizens testify it was simply a place of trade and not built to contain a slave block. This, possibly, is true of other places so marked in the South in order to attract the attention of Northern tourists.

Southern planters never, if it could be avoided, allowed their slaves to be sold at public outcry. It only happened when a man died without a will – then members of the family tried to buy the slaves in by families.

The only colony to forbid slaves was Georgia.

The first State to legislate against the slave trade was Georgia.

The first bill to allow a slaveholder to free his slaves was by Thomas Jefferson, of Virginia.

Jefferson urged in the Declaration of independence that the slave trade be forbidden. John Adams, of Massachusetts, urged that clause be omitted.

The only State that made it a felony to buy a slave was Virginia.

Thomas Jefferson insisted that Ohio, Illinois, Indiana, Michigan, and Wisconsin should not be slave States – and yet Virginia, a slave State, gave this territory.

A committee of five Virginians – Jefferson, Pendleton, Wythe, Mason and Thomas Lee – was appointed to revise the laws and prepare all slaveholders in the State for the gradual emancipation of their slaves. This law said all children born after the passage of the Act should be free, but must remain with their mothers until old enough to be self-supporting. Thirty-two times Virginia legislated against slavery.

Thomas Jefferson urged that all slaveholders free their slaves by gradual emancipation as soon as possible, for by the Missouri Compromise, where a State's right was interfered with by other States, he saw plainly that the day might come when sudden emancipation would take place, and he said "human nature shuddered at the prospect of it," but he thanked God he would not be alive to see it.

George Washington urged the gradual emancipation of his slaves and freed them by his will, and told Thomas Jefferson he wished all slaves could be freed.

George Mason believed in emancipation of his slaves and freed them.

John Randolph of Roanoke freed his slaves and bought territory in Ohio to place them after freedom. Zanesville, Ohio, where that large college for negroes is situated, is in that territory.

Henry Clay urged the gradual emancipation of the slaves.

Gen. Lee and his mother believed in gradual emancipation and practiced it, and so did many slaveholders at the South. Hundred of thousands of slaves had been freed in the South before 1820.

Jefferson Davis, when in the U.S. Senate, urged that a plan be made for emancipation that would be best for the slaveholders *and* the slave. This was why Southern men were so insistent about securing more slave territory to relieve the congested condition of the slave States that they might prepare the slaves as freed for their future government.

Abraham Lincoln said gradual emancipation was the best plan, and the North should not criticize too severely the Southern brethren for tardiness in this matter.

There were in the United States at one time 130 abolition societies – 106 were in the South – and 5/6 of the members of all were Southern slaveholders.

The Abolition Crusade which began at the time of the Missouri Compromise in 1820, and which reached an intense pitch in 1839, caused Southern men to withdraw membership in abolition societies.

The South has suffered greatly from misrepresentations in regard to the institution of slavery. History has grossly maligned, not only the institution, but the slaveholder. Cruelty as practiced in East Indies, the Barbadoes and elsewhere have been repeated and located in the South. One traveler declared he saw in his travels a negro in a cage exposed to wild birds and his eyes literally pecked out – and encyclopoedias and historians have located it in South Carolina. In the first place, there are no wild birds in South Carolina to have done the pecking, and in the second place, no Southern slaveholder would have stood for this for a moment.

The slaveholder has been accused of cruelty in separating mother and child on the slave block.

The selling of slaves in the South did not separate mother and child as often or with such cruelty as did the slave traffic in Africa – as did the hiding of the fugitive slave from their owners – as did the "Exodus Order" in Reconstruction days.

Southern States had very rigid laws along this line. In Louisiana, if a slaveholder separated mother and child, he must pay $1,000 and give up six of his slaves. Other States also had binding laws. We find, in the Massachusetts Continental Journal, March 1, 1778, an advertisement of a slave mother to be sold "with or without her six months' old child."

The Southern slaveholder has been accused of being responsible for the mulattoes in the South. The increase in mulattoes since freedom has been tenfold. There was no such thing as chattel slavery in the South.

White slavery in the North today is responsible for far more evils than ever came from the institution of slavery in the South.

The Southern planter has been accused of cruelty to his slaves – no cruelty on the part of any overseer can compare to that of the middle passage on the slave ships, where, on that long voyage, they were huddled as standing cattle and suffered from hunger and thirst so that they died by the hundreds.

Let it be remembered that no Southern man ever owned a slave ship. No Southern man ever commanded a slave ship. No Southern man ever went to Africa for slaves.

A Pittsburg, Pa., editor said, after hearing in Philadelphia a lecture on "The South of Yesterday":

"A sweet faced old lady delivered an address at the Bellevue Stratford Hotel in Philadelphia. She talked of the slaves of ante-bellum days to impress upon the younger generation of the South the fact that the slaves were well treated. The address was intended to try to obliterate sectional feeling. It is of importance to us today, for it affords contrast.

"As she spoke, the writer felt it justified the question: Are the white slaves today – those in industrial bondage – as well cared for as were the black slaves before the war? Is the industrial slave as well fed, as well clothed, as well housed as these black slaves were by their masters? Are the industrial slaves that work in the mills and mines and the sweat shops of today as well cared for as were the slaves of the South who worked in the field?

"And have thousands of the workingmen of Western Pennsylvania, after twenty-five years of labor, any more to show than the black slave after a corresponding term of service?"

Gen. Lee said, "There was no doubt that the blacks were immeasurably better off here than they were in Africa morally, physically and socially." He thought the freeing of them should be left in God's hands and not be settled by tempestuous controversy.

The South has been vilified for not educating the negro in the days of slavery.

The South was giving to the negro the best possible education – that education that fitted him for the workshop, the field, the church, the kitchen, the nursery, the home. This was an education that taught the negro self-control, obedience and perseverance – yes, taught him to realize his weaknesses and how to grow stronger for the battle of life. The institution of slavery, as it was in the South, so far from degrading the negro, was fast elevating him above his nature and his race.

We dared not teach the negroes on the plantations to read lest men of the John Brown type would urge them to rise, burn and kill our men, women and children on the plantation. Nat Turner, a free negro, did learn to read and was responsible for that insurrection in 1836 that resulted in the murder of sixty whites.

No higher compliment was ever paid the institution of slavery than that by the North, which was willing to make the negro its social and political equal after two hundred years of civilization under Southern Christianizing influence. Never has it been recorded in history such rapid civilization from savagery to Christian citizenship.

Charles E. Stowe said: "There must have been something in the institution of slavery of value to have produced such a beautiful Christian character as Uncle Tom" in his mother's book.

The South suffered under injustice and false representation in many, many ways.

In 1845, Southern Baptists were forced to withdraw from the Northern Baptists because they refused to accept a Southern slaveholder as a missionary.

The Southern Methodists, in 1844, were forced to separate because Bishop Andrews was not to be allowed to remain a Bishop as he had married a widow who owned slaves.

The Southern Presbyterians were forced to separate because a slaveholder was not allowed to partake of the communion.

The Episcopal Church continued united, but Bishop Elliott, of Georgia, in 1860, testified the church had suffered keenly from the misrepresentations of Northern brethren. He said:

"It is well for Christians and philanthropists to consider whether by their interference with the institution of slavery they may not be checking and impeding a work which is manifestly Providential. What if for ten generations the negroes have been slaves, if, through that Providence, they have been trained for future glory and independence, and for immortality?"

The black man ought to thank the institution of slavery – the easiest road that any slave people have ever passed from savagery to civilization with the kindest and most humane masters. Hundreds of thousands of the slaves in 1865 were professing Christians and many were partaking of the communion in the church of their masters.

All that the South wishes is justice. This she has never had. In all of her history she has never been an invader but a defender of rights.

John C. Calhoun said: "When did the South ever place her hand on the North? When did she ever interfere with her peculiar institutions? When did she ever aim a blow at her peace and security! When did she ever demand more than naked, sheer justice of the Union —" and this is all that the South asks for now.

CHAPTER THREE

☆　☆　☆　☆

How the Civilization of the Old South Was Destroyed

The XIII. Amendment in 1865 set free in the midst of their former owners nearly 6,000,000 slaves, totally unprepared for freedom, and while a factor, it was not the greatest factor in destroying the civilization of the South. The men of the Southern army returned to their desolated homes, having taken the oath of allegiance in good faith, and were ready to accept, without a murmur, this amendment when it came.

The planters began to parcel out their land and start their negroes in life as farm tenants. Their affection and interest in their negroes would not only have assured their protection but would have caused their being fed until self-supporting, and other Southern men would have also adjusted themselves to new conditions. Had they then been left untrammelled, matters would have been quickly adjusted. There might have been some friction, but far less than followed under reconstruction policies. The old masters would have helped their faithful negroes to buy homes and to prepare themselves for freedom. The negroes had confidence in their owners and would not have questioned their advice. They could have made better terms under these conditions than were made by false friends under the Freedman's Bureau.

The men of the South would not have given them civil or political rights until they were prepared for them. They would not have given them social equality, for this the negro did not desire, until false friends from the North urged it upon them as a right, and not even then, nor now, do the better class of negroes desire it. The negroes would have been given school opportunities and an education befitting the race would have been given to them. They would not have been given instruction in Greek and Latin and higher mathematics, except to those desiring to teach and to preach, but the majority would have been prepared for life along industrial lines.

The North, at this time, blundered greatly by allowing Thad Stevens and his Committee to issue the "Exodus Order" which separated the negroes from their old owners, and to place in the South the Freedman's Bureau with the promise of "forty acres and a mule" – encouraging shiftlessness!

This unwise policy was the real blow aimed at the overthrow of the civilization of the Old South. The men of the South were then put under military discipline which actually tied their hands, and only the Ku Klux, the "Chivalry of the Old South," could break these bonds that fettered them.

The negroes began rapidly to leave their homes, because they had been told that they would be kept in slavery still if they did not. Strange negroes came in their stead and the trouble began – for, by the Freedman's Bureau, the part of the negro was always taken against the whites, whether right or wrong. Men and women who never had done menial work now had to learn, rather than contend with impertinent negroes they had no power to punish. Many had no money to pay for help. and the negroes had no desire to work. They were waiting for some one to support them.

The South blundered in allowing the North to supply the teachers for the negro schools. These teachers should have been the white people or the negroes of the South.

"School marms" came down, impressed with the missionary spirit, to help these "poor benighted blacks," to keep them from being downtrodden and imposed upon, and they gave to them a taste of social equality which spoiled them for service in Southern homes.

One of these teachers invited "Aunt Mandy," calling her Mrs. Brown, to come in to sit with her, saying she was lonely.

"Are you going'?" asked Ole Mis'.

"Law, Ole Mis', you know I aint goin'! Them white folks that wants me to set with them aint the white folks I wants to set with."

This was the thought of the aristocratic negro of the Old South.

Mammy, being told that Pres. Roosevelt had invited Booker Washington to lunch with him, said, "Surely Booker Washington had better manners than to set down to the white folks' table?"

"No, he didn't, Mammy, he went in and took lunch with Mr. Roosevelt."

"Oh! I am 'shamed of Booker Washington – his mammy ought to have taught him better manners than that."

"But, Mammy, suppose it had been you, and Pres. Roosevelt had insisted upon it, what would you have said?"

"Oh! I would have said, 'Scuse me, Mars Roosevelt, I ain't hongry."

And that is just the answer a Southern negro aristrocrat would have made. They had an aristocracy just as marked as the whites had, and this aristocracy the whites respected.

Rena was asked to take dinner at the University where her daughter received her diploma. She accepted the invitation, but when she found that she was to sit at the table with the white members of the faculty, she slipped out of the room, saying, "My little nigger can eat with white folks, but I can't."

The helplessness of the negro at the time of freedom was pathetic. He was a little child in his dependence. He had no need for money, for he once had supplied to him the things money would buy for his needs, so when he received his money for wages he spent it as a child.

The first driver my father was forced to hire, a year after the surrender, had to be furnished a suit of clothes and hat and shoes before he was presentable on the carriage seat. Yet when he was paid his first month's wages of $10, $8 was spent for an accordion and the remaining $2 for fire crackers, which like a child he quickly fired.

A Northern man who bought one of the Southern plantations noticed an old negro man helping himself to fire wood. He asked him one day where he bought his wood.

"It's jest this way," he answered, "My pa was coachman at the Big House over there, and he pa and he pa – so there's no need for one gentleman to ax another gentleman whar he gits his wood." Ole Marster had always given his wood so this old negro had no idea he was stealing.

That wood was his by right of service from his family was the teaching of the carpetbaggers after the war. To steal from a negro was a great sin, they said, but no sin to steal from white people, for all they had the negroes made. The Southern people suffered grievously from this teaching. They saw with real distress how, under false teaching, the negroes were being alienated from them and being harmed, not helped. The negroes under false advisers resented any interference from Southern whites, and the situation became terrible – far worse than is pictured in "The Birth of a Nation," horrible as that is. It was not only a time of real oppression, but also a time of repression, suppression and fearful humiliation. The South lost $2,000,000,000 by loss of slaves, together with confiscated and destroyed property. The South was also left with a bonded war debt of $300,000,000.

It is really refreshing to realize, even at this late day, that some of the leading negro leaders are conscious of the mistakes that have been made and are willing to acknowledge it.

A leader named Wilkins, at Little Rock, Ark., in 1915, said on Emancipation Day:

"We are foolish for celebrating an event which has meant nothing to us but humiliation, persecution, alienation, degradation, obloquy, scorn, and contempt.

"We are celebrating a day that never took place and you know it as well as I do.

"But some things did take place on that day. Our Southern white friends fed us, clothed us, and administered to us. Let us not forget that, but rather celebrate that. Remember now, those of you who think Lincoln's Proclamation set us free, that if it did, it was our white friends that kept us from starving."

Pres. Lincoln's Emancipation Proclamation never freed the negro nor did Lincoln expect it to. It was a political move against the seceding States to force men at the North to re-enlist, and in the hope that it would make Southern men return to protect their families from negro insurrection and thus end the war, and to induce foreign nations to refuse to acknowledge the Confederacy.

Not a negro in the States that did not secede was freed by Lincoln's Proclamation and it had no effect even in the South as it was unconstitutional and Lincoln knew it. Many in the North resented it, and Lincoln was unhappy over the situation as Lamon testified. The negroes were freed by an amendment offered by a Southern man and did not become a law until after Lincoln's death. It really is a farce for negroes to celebrate Emancipation Day.

By the freedom of the slaves and the estrangements that followed between them and their former owners the civilization of the Old South gradually passed away.

Mark Twain said, "The eight years in America, 1860-1868, uprooted an institution centuries old, and wrought so profoundly upon the national character of the people that the influence will be felt for two or three generations." Mark Twain was a Southern man and knew what he was talking about.

Chas. E. Stowe, the son of Harriet Beecher Stowe, said: "If you ask me if the slaves were better off under the institution of slavery than they are under freedom, I must, in candor, answer that some were better off for they were not fit for freedom."

Again he said: "If slavery was an unutterably evil institution, how can you account for the faithfulness of the negroes on the plantations when the men were at the front, and no act of violence known among them?"

Senator Vance said, "The negro has made more progress in one hundred years as a Southern slave than in all the three thousand years intervening from his creation until his landing on these shores." (Dowd's *Life of Vance*, p. 253.)

Gen. Armstrong, a Northern man, said: "While slavery in the South was called the sum of all villainies, it became the greatest missionary enterprise of the century."

When the slaves were freed, we turned them over to the North an orderly, fairly industrious race, practically without disease or crime, and the North felt they were worthy of social and political equality, and so legislated.

The negroes then were one-half the population of the South. The statistics in regard to illiteracy at the South has greatly vilified the South because in the statistics were the 6,000,000 slaves who, with few exceptions, could read or write.

At the surrender, the South had nothing but the ground upon which to stand, and yet began to be heavily taxed to educate this mass of blacks as well as the whites. Justice has never been given the South for what she did at this time and what she is still doing.

Read Winthrop Talbot's article in the December *North American Review* (1915), and see what part of the country has the brand of illiteracy today. It will be found that the New England States, the Middle States, and the Northern States are the sufferers under present statistics regarding illiteracy.

The South, according to the statistics of 1911, had spent on the negro $120,000,000 for education. (Report of Dr. Harris, Commissioner of Education.) That sum has largely increased in the six years that have followed.

What progress has the negro made in those fifty years? He has as a race, (note that I say *as a race,*) become disorderly, idle, vicious and diseased. There are three times more criminals among them today than among the uneducated native whites; one-half more criminals than among the foreign whites, and 7/10 of the negro criminals are under thirty years of age – so slavery can in no wise be held responsible for that.

When such abuse comes from the North about lynching and crimes in the South, do they realize that only 1/60 of the population of the North is negro, while more than 1/2 in the South is negro, and in many localities in the South it is

9/10 negro. Isn't it radically unfair to bring the charges upon violation of mob law in Georgia – and I am not defending mob law – I think it awful wherever found – when they never seem to realize that the home of mob law was in New England and other Northern States?

Was not Garrison dragged by a mob in the streets of Boston?

Did not New Englanders mob officers of the National Government for trying to enforce the law?

Wasn't Lovejoy put to death by a mob in Boston?

Did not New Yorkers massacre men, women and children and burn nineteen negroes? Was a negro ever burned in a Southern State?

Was not Philadelphia the home of mobs at one time?

Did not a mob burn an orphanage in Philadelphia and kill women and children?

Was not a negro chained and burned at Wilmington, Delaware?

Was not a negro hanged by a mob before the court-house door at Urbana, Ohio?

Did not a mob with dynamite bombs defy the police in Chicago and not one offender brought to justice?

Will those newspapers so unjust to Georgia, and to the South as a whole, look into those mobs at Akron and Springfield, Ohio; Danville and Springfield, Illinois; Evansville and Rockport, Indiana; and Coatsville, Pennsylvania, and in States much nearer to them than Georgia? Will they not inquire into statistics and truthfully find out, if they are honest enough to admit it, that there have been more mobs proportionally to negro population in the North than in the South, and most of the violation of mob law is because of the negro!

They ask continually, "What's the matter with Georgia?" I can tell them the matter, for I am a Georgian. Georgia is surpassing those States so rapidly in prosperity that the eye of political jealousy is fastened on her.

The South is willing to be just and give to all justice, but she will ever resent injustice – and the cry against the South in regard to this matter is gross injustice. The *Chicago Tribune* said, "The South is a region of illiteracy, blatant self righteousness, and unless new blood is infused in the South it will continue to be a menace to the American Nation." My, where did this editor come from? He must be related to Medill of Chicago, who Lincoln said caused him to declare war, by arming Fort Sumter. There are some in the North who wish to deprive the South of the right to manage any of her own affairs.

Pres. Wilson sees a great danger to the South coming from this tendency to a centralized government and stands squarely for State Rights. The South, under present conditions, cannot afford to surrender her State rights. If she should, a worse than Reconstruction Period would follow, and no Ku Klux can protect her.

The North disfranchised the illiterate Indians, the illiterate yellow man, the illiterate negroes in her midst before the war, yet, after the war, the North enfranchised 6,000,000 illiterate negroes in the South. This was not just.

Has the negro as a race been benefitted by freedom? Now understand I said *as a race*. Unhesitatingly, no!

While the educated negro has made rapid progress and some have accomplished great things for which they deserve high commendation; some have accumulated much property; some have built good homes; some are well to do; some have made good citizens and some have made good teachers, good preachers, good physicians, good dentists, good dressmakers – and some are training their children well – but, take them as a race, they are undoubtedly weaker today physically, morally and religiously.

The negroes are realizing this and are

grieving over it. They are fast decreasing as a race while the white is fast increasing.

The white race on the other hand is decidedly better off since freedom; it is the negro which has suffered from sudden emancipation. The South has never been so prosperous as it is today, showing what an incubus slavery was upon the slaveholder.

Just as in 1820 the eyes of political jealousy were turned upon the Slave States because of their prosperity and prominence in the control of the affairs of the government, and State Rights were aimed at by the Missouri Compromise, so today the eyes of political jealousy are again turned to the South because of its unparalleled prosperity and prominence in government affairs, and a combined effort is being made to destroy State Rights, and the surprise is that many Southern men and women are abetting the movement.

We of the South – as much as we have been forced to bear from the impertinent and shiftless negro of freedom – can never and must never forget the faithful negroes of slavery. In my volume of "Tributes to Faithful Slaves" I have some very touching incidents that have come under my own personal observation.

I was in Lexington, Va., and, on entering the gate of the cemetery, I saw a monument to

DAVID McKINLY erected by PETER FLEMING, HIS FORMER SLAVE. Peter returned to his old home, after many years, to find his old master dead, and the family not able to put a monument over him, so he asked permission of the family to order a monument and to pay for it himself.

Near to Stonewall Jackson's monument in the same cemetery in a lot the master and slave sleep side by side, "awaiting the Resurrection."

"To the memory of SAMUEL HAYS in loving remembrance for faithful service this stone is erected by the desire of his master."

In another lot side by side with her mistress "ELIZA SMITH A FAITHFUL SERVANT" sleeps.

When at Petersburg, Va., in the Old Blanford Cemetery, I saw there another monument among the whites erected to "A BELOVED OLD MAMMY."

An old ex-slave was found in Washington City hunting for "Mars Sherman" because "Mis' Clio," his "Mistis," had told him to thank Gen. Sherman for not burning her home at Cartersville, Ga.

"Mis' Clio," from Augusta, Ga., had been Gen. Sherman's sweetheart when he was at West Point. When the old negro heard that Sherman had been dead many years, he burst into tears, saying, "I promised Mis' Clio to thank him."

As long as one of the old regime lived they were always so polite, so humble, so proud, so loyal, so true. Few there are that still remain.

Let us then, the children and grandchildren of the men who wore the gray, stretch out a kindly hand to the children and grandchildren of those who were the faithful protectors of our mothers and grandmothers in the days that tried men's souls, and make them to understand that we want them in the South, and that the South is their logical home, and that understanding each other as we do, we can work for the things that are best for both races.

They are fast realizing that they cannot accomplish anything worth while without the sympathy and co-operation of the white people of the South. The faithfulness of their forefathers has never been surpassed in the annals of servitude, and those faithful ones had no part in bringing about the present state of affairs.

The good will between the races – white and black – in the South must be rebuilt upon the foundation laid in the days of slavery. This foundation was severely shaken by the storm that beat upon us in Reconstruction days and the days that followed. Let us hope that it has not been wholly destroyed.

At Fort Mill, S.C., Capt. S.E. White erected the first monument to faithful slaves – no doubt, many more will be erected throughout the South.

At every Confederate Reunion, some of the old slaves who went with their masters into camp to wait on them and forage for them are still to be seen. Every opportunity was given these negroes to cross the lines to the enemy. Has any such desertion been recorded? Every slaveholder that was able to bear expenses was allowed to take his valet with him to the army.

"The Birth of a Nation" will do much to enable the white people of the South to right a wrong to the negroes, for the negroes represented there, with the exception of old Mammy, were not our faithful negroes that guarded our homes. but they were the bad runaway negroes that had fallen under the influence of the carpetbagger and the scalawag, and to whom had been given guns to kill and destroy, and I do not wonder that the negroes resent the Play for these young negroes of today know nothing of the history of those times. I would like to tell them about it, for I lived then and know the truth.

The adjustment period was fearful in the South, and was another great factor in destroying the old civilization. The women of the Old South were forced then to learn, not only to cook, to wash and iron, but to do the most menial forms of household drudgery. The kitchen in the Old South was never attached to the house. Water had to be drawn from a well or brought from a spring, often entailing labor and great inconvenience, for waterworks were unknown, and wood stoves were just introduced, very few were able to possess one before the war. The cooking was largely done in open fireplaces, with pot hooks and ovens, so wood had to be cut and ashes cleared away. Tallow candles and lightwood knots and, occasionally, sperm candles for company, and lard lamps were the dependence for lights – so all of these things had to be adjusted.

So many men, the heads of the house, had been killed in battle or died in prison. How could the mother, in the kitchen away from the house, continue to gather the children for family prayers?

How could hospitality, for which the Old South was so noted, continue under such changed conditions – with no servants to do the work, and often no money to hire any or to buy necessary provisions?

The education of the children was taken from the home and private schools to the public schools. There had been no public schools under the old regime in the South. A Southern gentle-

man resented having the State educate his child
– but the changed condition forced this upon him,
and it humiliated him. Free schools in the South
had been only for those too poor to pay tuition or
to employ a tutor.

How could the husband rushing off to his
business office, and children rushing off to
school, keep up that conversation around the
family board so conducive to culture?

Adjustment to new conditions came gradually. The kitchen became a part of the house; the
introduction of waterworks relieved the labor of
drawing the water; gas and electric stoves and the
fireless cooker make now the preparation of
meals a less perplexing question; gas and elec-
tricity have revolutionized the light situation; so
the women of the South today are as independent
as their Northern sisters and far ahead of them in
dealing with colored help, for say what you will,
the women of the South knowing the weaknesses
of these people can better sympathize with them,
and they do treat them with far more consider-
ation than the people of other sections. There is
no doubt that the negro finds his truest friends in
the South, and that, too, with no social equality
ideas to upset him.

Again, Wilkins said: "There would have
been no friction between the Southern people and

the negroes, if left alone. The friction came from the carpetbaggers who came to alienate us from our friends and teach us impossible ambitions. When he had secured his ill-gotten gains, he left leaving us to meet the storm of an outraged manhood."

CHAPTER FOUR

☆ ☆ ☆ ☆

What Has Replaced the Civilization of the Old South

The civilization of today in its achievements, it must be admitted, is broader; its prospects are brighter, more steadfast and more buoyant.

The slaves are free, but the slaveholders rejoice over it. The responsibility of caring for them, physically, morally and religiously, was very great. But while they rejoice over their freedom they have never felt the method of freeing them was just, because it was unconstitutional. The slaveholders of the South are the only ones recorded in history who have had their slaves taken from them by force of arms without full compensation. I feel sure the day will come when the North will right this wrong. I believe Abraham Lincoln would have urged it had he lived, for he realized the Constitution had not been violated by the South, and he planned to let the seceding States into the Union on very easy terms, and he really wished Pres. Davis to escape.

The civilization of the Old South was very different from the civilization of today. There was leisure then to think, to read and to meditate. There was time to be thoughtful of others, to be courteous, to be polite. In this rushing life of today we have lost the social graces, the charming manners, the art of letter writing, he gift of conversation. It is now hurry, hurry to keep up with the telegraph, the telephone, the type writer, the phonograph, the automobile, the moving picture shows, yes, and the flying machine, too.

The civilization of today is one of fearful activity. The rush and grind of work is wearing out the human frame. Men and women are being dwarfed physically, and I fear morally, and are dying at an earlier age.

We have no time to study the ethics of life. We no longer are polite enough, chivalrous enough. The newspapers are vying with each other to secure the most sensational story, and draw attention to it by the largest headlines. The owners of newspapers and magazines say this is absolutely necessary in order to secure subscribers – they must have what the public demands. Isn't that fearful! This throws the responsibility upon the reader more than upon the editor or owner.

The managers of moving picture shows feel they must have some indecent representation in order to attract a crowd. They must have what the public demands. Isn't that fearful! This throws the responsibility upon you who encourage these indecent representations more than upon the owner of the film.

The youth of our land are losing modesty and the sense of propriety. There is a lamentable familiarity between the sexes.

Boys calling girls by their first names on first introduction and girls allowing it. Boys smoking cigarettes on the street while walking with girls, and girls allowing it. We had no chewing gum and tooth pick brigades in the Old South.

The books on our library table and on our book shelves are far from being pure and true, and are leading our young people to have false views of life, and parents seem indifferent to it. Girls are needing the guidance and watchcare of good mothers as never before.

Social entertainments given by women and girls are ruling out men and boys. The consequence is the men and boys are awkward in ladies' presence, and are lacking in old time chivalry. They keep their hats on in the presence of ladies; they sit when elders enter the room; they smoke in the presence of ladies without asking permission – they smoke while walking with ladies, and in the dining rooms of hotels; they fail to give their seats on cars or trains to standing women or to aged men; they are fast losing the little courtesies of life which made the old civilization so beautiful and attractive.

The women and girls are much to blame for this for they are not demanding these things from the men and boys, but really act sometimes so as not to deserve any thing better. Our girls are growing bolder and less modest by trying to be mannish. They are seeking the men instead of making the men seek them as in the days of yore. Ole Mis' daughters kept their lovers waiting a long time to get the prize well worth the having, and then there was no changing the mind afterwards.

It really is a selfish age – every man for himself is the rule of this day, and little thought of the one left behind in the race of life.

do you ask "Is there no chivalry in the land today?" Has it all passed away?

There certainly is chivalry today. Thank God it has not all passed away. I know of many homes where chivalry is not dead.

In Richmond, Virginia, a few days ago, a Confederate veteran, very old and feeble, was tenderly assisted into a jitney by a young driver with the air of a Lord Chesterfield. When the old man fumbled for his nickel, and was mortified that he could not find it, the young man – with old time chivalry – said: "No *matter about the nickel, you paid your fare years ago!"*

What could have been more chivalrous?

At the Reunion at Birmingham I failed to find a taxi and was forced to catch the street car with two large valises. I was greatly distressed as to what I should do when the station was reached. Quickly two boy scouts rushed up and kindly took the valises to the train. When I insisted upon some compensation for their aid it was persistently refused with, "It is a pleasure to be of assistance to an old lady." No, chivalry is not dead.

A street car conductor made a crowd of young and middle aged stand back until he had gallantly aided an old lady to enter the car. I was the "old lady." Wasn't that chivalrous?

There is no purity in politics today! Under the old civilization, bribery and corruption was treated with scorn and derision. The office sought the man, not the man the office. Now, no man can gain office without money being used by or against him.

Ole Marster's sons could not be bribed, and Ole Marster's sons paid their debts. Ole Marster's sons did not lie or steal or cheat or take or give an insult without demanding reparation. Duelling, it is true, was an evil of the old civilization which has passed away rightfully.

Sometimes merchants under the old regime need not give their note for a bill of goods – their word was as good as their bond. It is not so today.

Ole Mis' daughters were charming, gracious and lovable. They made faithful wives, devoted mothers, noted housekeepers; they were pillars of the church, good neighbors, considerate mistresses, kind and generous to the poor.

Do we care, today, if our home is not a religious home?

Our grandmothers did! It was considered a dreadful thing if it were not.

Do we care if our servants, today, are not religious, and do not live moral lives?

Our grandmothers did, and used all influence to help them to make their lives right.

I know one family today where the mistress of the home reads the Bible daily to the servants as her mother did, and asks them into family prayers – but this, I fear, is a rare exception.

Even God's blessing is being omitted from the daily meals in many homes.

We miss the "table talk" of those olden days where children were seen not heard, and where our elders discussed politics, religion, literature, music or art. Today gossip, scandal, coarse jokes or poor servants are the themes of conversation at the table. We were taught in the old days if we had nothing good to say of a person to say nothing at all.

Today the family rarely gathers at the family altar or the family board. The men rush off to business, the girls and boys have spent the night in dancing and frolicing and so must turn day into night. The children rush from the dining table to the moving picture show. Clubs are taking the men from home at night and women from home in the day. The servant question has driven the housewives to light house-keeping, and apartment and hotel life. The old fireside is fast passing away!

One may ask: "Do you really think the world is getting more wicked day by day?"

No, I do not. We are hearing more quickly of the wickedness. There are more people in the world today – and daily newspapers abound. I really believe more people are studying God's

Word today than ever before. More are more keenly interested in missionary enterprises and have a deeper love and sympathy in their hearts for their brother man. More philanthropic works are being carried on in the world than ever before. We had no Laymen's Movements, no Young Men's or Young Women's Christian Associations as we have now, doing a wonderful work.

Deference to woman has always heretofore been a distinguishing characteristic of the Southern people. Deference to woman today cannot be said to be the distinguishing characteristics of the Southern people. How have we lost out? It is quite time to ask this question and to remedy the evil if possible. To me it is deplorable.

The adjustments that had to be made in the home, in the State, in the country after the War between the States caused a complete uprooting of all customs and ways of living and thinking and even after fifty years we still are suffering from this uprooting in the South.

When slavery was destroyed, the women in the South had to enter the field of labor – a thing unheard of in the days of the Old South. Woman has had to think faster, act more circumspectly to defend herself from insult and injustice as so many defenders of women in the South gave their lives on the field of battle. This has made our women less gracious, but more independent. Organizations for women by women were not needed before the war, save in church work, but are now badly needed to meet present conditions. The women in Club work have met and are still meeting fearful needs of today. Patriotic organizations are needed to keep alive the spirit of patriotism in the hearts of the young people in the land. We must teach them loyalty to our government, and to our country's flag, to our State and our State flag, to our city and all that pertains to civic righteousness. We must teach our Southern children also reverence for the *Stars and Bars,* that flag under which their Confederate fathers fought four years for the rights they knew were theirs, and for a cause that was never lost.

The new civilization has made great progress in health statistics. Sanitation is being perfected, and epidemics have been largely mastered, so that many localities in the South once uninhabitable during certain seasons of the year are now actually health resorts. And while this may be said, there have undoubtedly arisen many diseases unknown before that possibly have come from too much germ extinction. Who can tell? Scientists are now studying this question.

Instead of the South producing great political leaders as she did under the life on the old plantation, she is, today, producing men of science, great inventors, men of large business affairs. Southern men have made Panama habitable; they have stamped out the yellow fever and by sanitary regulations controlled many diseases.

Southern men gave ether as an anaesthetic and made surgery possible in hospital service, suggested the hypodermic needle and Southern men were first to have a hospital for women and first to perform an operation on the heart, and first to remove the appendix, and first to manufacture ice.

Southern men have tunnelled the Hudson, planned great canals and dams and suggested the River and Flood system.

Southern men have been and are still great railroad magnates and a man of the South was first to suggest a railroad commission.

Southern men were first to suggest wireless telegraphy, if Marconi did perfect it; first to make an XRay apparatus, if the Germans did suggest it; first to use a telephone, if Bell did seize the thought and carry it to completion; first to have a typesetter, if others have perfected it.

It was Southern men who first suggested a quarantine station, and also to suggest a weather bureau, even if Abbe has perfected it.

It was Southern men who suggested an iron-clad vessel and a sounding apparatus.

It was Southern men who suggested the rural delivery and how to cup the trees for resin.

I don't believe you know that the largest cotton factory in the world under one roof is in South Carolina!

The hottest Artesian wells in the world are in Texas.

The largest cotton warehouse in the world is in Tennessee.

The largest canning factory in the world is in Arkansas.

The largest lumber mill in the United States is in Louisiana.

The largest oil fields are in Texas, and Oklahoma.

The largest floating dry docks in the world are in Maryland.

The largest maganese mines in the world are in Virginia.

The largest lead mines in the world are in Missouri.

The largest commercial lock in the world is in Alabama.

The Mississippi River with its tributaries is the largest river in the world.

The largest cave in the world is in Kentucky.

The largest shippers of strawberry plants in the world are in North Carolina.

The oldest church in the United States is in Florida.

The largest sulphuric acid plant in the world is in Tennessee, and Georgia has more sulphuric acid plants than any other State. Think what fertilizers mean to the farmers of today.

The largest bauxite mines in the world are in Arkansas, and 90% of the world's production is there. Think what aluminum is meaning to the world today!

The greatest mountain of stone in the world is in Georgia – a geological monstrosity seven miles in circumference and one and one-half miles high. The perpendicular side of it is to be dedicated to Confederate valor. That will be the greatest monument in the world – a memorial to the bravest soldiers who ever marched to battle!

It has been said, "The Confederacy went down in defeat." If that be true, why does the Confederate soldier wear the Cross of Honor which is worn only by the VICTOR?

If that be true, why are more monuments erected to the Confederate soldier than to any other soldier that ever fought in any other war?

Monuments are not usually erected to the defeated.

If that be true, why is the greatest monument in the world being erected to commemorate Confederate valor?

No, the cause for which the Confederate soldier fought was in no sense a "Lost Cause," but a great VICTORY which will go sounding down the ages.

The Confederate soldiers stood for a cause they knew to be right. Their leader, Jefferson Davis, was never convicted of either treason or rebellion. The trial which he demanded, over and over again, was refused him and the case stands today upon the records in the United States Supreme Court, there to remain forever, and the Cause for which he stood is vindicated in the eyes of the world, by the written testimony of *those who fought against him.*

Our manufacturing industries are now on a large scale. Cotton is still King, but other industries are about to dethrone King Cotton.

The South was first to diversify crops and the State that first did it was Georgia.

The South, today, is far more prosperous than ever before. We are beginning to know more fully our possibilities. We are learning to utilize our own resources, and are less dependent upon other sections and other countries.

We speak of the South. Do we realize what is meant by it? A section of 989,167 square miles, as much territory as all of the German Empire, Norway, Sweden, Italy, Switzerland, France Spain, Belgium, Holland and Great Britain combined, with a population of over 112,000,000.

The War between the States taught us of the South our unpreparedness. The war in Europe is teaching our whole nation our unpreparedness. Thank God for President Wilson – a man of peace and a man of vision!

The Revolutionary War brought Cavalier and Puritan together in a common love of country, so we, today, North, South, East and West are being brought more closely together than ever before as true Americans under one flag and loyal to a Democratic Government with State Sovereignty stressed.

We must be ready, after this war ends, to lend a helping hand to all nations needing help, for no blessing will come to us if we allow selfishness to engulf us.

Remember that this civilization that has replaced the old civilization rests with you and me whether it shall be a better civilization or not. Upon the individual man and woman in this country rests a fearful responsibility. Shall our influence – unconscious influence, which is the strongest – be for the upbuilding or the pulling down of this great Nation which God has entrusted into our keeping. God grant that we shall one and all stand ever on the side of RIGHT.

APPENDIX

The Ante-Bellum Southern Woman
by Miss Winnie Davis

Since the day of exploded ideals has arrived, when William Tell and George Washington's little hatchet – yea, even the all-pervading Puritan who dominated our school histories – one and all have been dethroned from their sure seats, it seems as if the traditional Southern woman of the old plantation life might be allowed to descend from the cross where she has been nailed for generations.

This graceful but lackadaisical effigy of the imaginary "Southern Princess," who alternately lolled in a hammock in slothful self-indulgence, or arose in her wrath to scourge her helpless dependents, is the creation which our neighbors have been pleased to call the "typical Southern woman."

How different was the real housemistress who, on the great river properties, before the war, ruled the destinies of her family with gentle and wise sway. To us who know her in her old age it seems inexplicable that her place has been so long usurped by the figure fashioned by a hostile sculptor.

What a blessing this woman is to the "New South," the South of struggles and poverty – even the bitterest of her detractors must acknowledge, now that the clouds and smoke of battle begin to clear away and under the sun of peace reveal her true self.

What she was in the larger and more complicated sphere of her old life is known only to those who took part in it, or to the younger generation who feel the beneficent influence of her character. Had the women of the plantations been the lazy drones of the popular fancy, dreaming away their aimless lives in an atmosphere heavy with the odors of yellow jasmine, magnolias and roses, she would have been vanquished by the conditions over which she has been victorious. When war, pestilence, famine settled on her country the Southern woman, armed cap-a-pie with her heredity of good housewifery, self-control and patience, sprung uncomplaining and cheerful to her place, and vanquished her difficulties with a manly vigor and a womanly grace, the memory of which is very precious and sweet savored to those with whom she dwelt.

She probably did not understand the higher mathematics, but her arithmetic sufficed for household accounts and to gauge her expenses.

Her family practice in the hospital of her plantation made her the best of nurses.

Although her ideas of modern philosophy may have been of the vaguest, gentle and sincere piety breathed through all her arduous life, and made of her the best model for the half-civilized souls intrusted to her care, and also exerted refining influence over the men of her family.

If among the Hebrews each man was a priest to his own family, among our people every woman officiated as priestess in the isolated corner where she dwelt with the man toward whom "duty was pleasure and love was law," to whom "for better or worse," until death should them part. With her whole heart she gave her best energies to his service. It was her mission to counsel and comfort the weak-hearted and succor all those who were desolate and distressed, were they of her own or of the subject race. She was the mediatrix, the teacher, and in short the mother of her people; and to her, if to anyone, the negro owes his present civilization and moral culture. The prejudices of her male relatives were arrayed against publicity of any kind for her – even the homage due to her virtues seemed an invasion of the sanctity of home. Thus the record of her deeds has been suppressed, and she blossomed, bore noble fruit, and faded behind a screen so thick that it has obscured to the outside world the gracious lines of her personality, and her works alone praised her "in the gates," but her children now rise up and call her blessed.

To understand the so-called "New South," it is necessary to comprehend the actual duty of her mothers and the social relations which brought forth a race of people honorable, kindly, faithful and recklessly brave, yet adaptable in the highest degree.

These positive virtues are not generally associated with adaptability to new conditions, yet the Southern people in their bitter experience of defeat have given evidence of this power in its full significance.

The men and women of our country had, during the slave-holding period, fulfilled so many varying and incongruous duties to their slaves that they were in a measure fitted for any labor. The first lesson that a little Southern girl learned, in preparation of her duties as mistress of a plantation, was her association, usually developing into a warm friendship, with the maid of her own age, who was generally given by the mother of the negro to "be some sarvice to little missie," a sort of counterpart to the "body servant" whom the recent dialect stories have made so familiar to our non-slaveholding neighbors. Although the peculiar relations of things made this intimacy less close between master and man, the love which began in their early youth ripened generally into a hearty affection which usually was lifelong, beginning, as it did, with their childish games in the negro quarter.

It is doubtful if there was ever a *terre defevdus* so attractive to a child as this same "quarter," a collection of small dwellings built on each side of a street, and inhabited by children of a larger growth who were prodigal of stories flavored by the faith of the *raconteur.* There were friendly yellow dogs; chickens, ruffled, muffled and duck-legged, which answered to names, with callow broods racing after them, and wonderful hens' nests full of eggs in unfrequented corners; fires in the open air with fat sweet potatoes roasting in their ashes; doll baby gardens planted and torn up at once by a multitude of little coffee-colored playmates who scampered about "little missus" in a frenzy of delight.

Mistress and maiden confided everything to each other, and their mutual affection stood the mistress in good stead in her afterlife and enabled her often to penetrate the interesting but bewildering tangle of "tergiversations" which the plantation negro calls his thoughts. Experience taught her the habit of their minds, and opened to her the genuine dialect of a thousand idioms which she would afterward have to use in instructing her slaves. It also initiated her into the African standards of right and wrong, by which she gauged the depth of the offender's culpability.

There, too, she learned the potentiality of sarcasm in dealing with a race so alive to a sense of the ludicrous that an appeal to its risibles will often answer the purpose better than punishment.

An instance of this kind is given of a Southern woman who cured her negro marketman of bringing the family a turkey daily for dinner because he had speculated in them and they were cheaper than other meat. She invited him to "stand on the gallery and gobble a little." This ludicrous performance deterred him from a repetition of his offense when more serious remonstrance had proved fruitless.

The little girls were present at all the milkings, churnings, and even the grinding of meat on the place, and so became familiar with the minutia of these industries.

When the young mistress was married the superintendence of these duties devolved upon her – the curing of the meat, which was to form the staple food of the white and black family throughout the year, the recipes for which were handed down from mother to daughter for generations. As there were no markets, chickens and turkeys and ducks and geese must be reared in plenty; butter must be churned; a good vegetable garden sedulously cultivated; the fruit trees and berry vines persuaded to bear fruit after their kind; to overlook the weaving-room, where the cotton cloths as well as woolen used to be made, was also her duty; and in all these things our grandmothers and mothers were as proficient as the chatelaines of the Middle Ages. Much of these arts the Southern child absorbed without special instruction. Also a part of her education was the cutting and sewing of all kinds of garments, the cooking and serving of all sorts of dainties, and the intelligent care of the sick.

This practical education went hand in hand with the elementary and theoretical one under governesses, or in the little schools composed of the children of the neighboring places.

Whether this method of mixing the actual

with the ideal was peculiarly beneficial to their minds, or that the loneliness of their lives drove them into more serious studies, it is remarkable how many well-read women there were on these river places whose familiarity with the classics was close enough to be loving, and whose skill in the tinkling music of their day was of no mean proficiency.

So well was their capacity and attainments recognized that the distinguished American historian of this century, Mr. Bancroft, declined a wager with a Southern lady about a literary question, saying: "I have been told to beware of the plantation woman – she reads so many books she will prove me in the wrong."

As the Southern woman developed into maturity, dividing her time between her studies and observation of the busy life around her, she read in the daily practice of her elders the constantly repeated lesson of her duty to her sable dependents.

On the plantation it was not a question of cottage visiting, such as is common in English and New England country life. It was the actual care of an irresponsible family, large and often refractory enough to dampen the zeal of the most philanthropic.

There were clothes to be made for the babies and little children, and as well for the "or-phans," the shiftless bachelors and motherless boys and girls who would not sew if they could. Then the seamstresses who were to do this work were to be trained from the manner of holding a needle and scissors through all the various kinds of stitches to be taken up to dressmaking.

There were waiters, waitresses and dairy maids to instruct and cooks to superintend. Also there must be many of these skilled servants, because, without exception, they all had families, and if one of these should be taken ill another servant must be taken out of the field to supply the parent's place in the house, so that the child might be properly attended and the mother's heart at ease.

The fallacy that those darky servants grew like blackberries on the briers belongs to that land of Cockagne where roasted pigeons fell from the sky. Certainly these self-producing prodigies did not exist for our mothers. It will be only after a long and careful course of training, with mutual forbearance and patience, that the free negro will make as accomplished a servant as our slaves were.

The extreme penalty of whipping was reserved for such offenses as stealing and other crimes. As the negroes could not be "discharged without a character," the mistress was not armed with the terror always in the hands of the modern housewife, but she had to make the best of her husband's negroes as she found them, trusting to her own powers as educator to form of the young ones such servants as she would like to have about her.

To sell one of the negroes "born on the place" was an evidence of the direst poverty of the master or of the most heinous conduct on the part of the slave.

Such peccadilloes as insubordination, untidiness or stupidity formed no reason to the mind of either mistress or maid in the "Old South" for a dissolution of their mutual relation; nor could a tormented mistress find relief by giving a useless servant her freedom.

There is an authentic story of one who tried, during a visit to the North, to thus rid herself of a drunken maid whose taste for Madeira had tempted her to run up a score on her mistress' account at the neighboring drinking shop. When the mistress remonstrated the negro answered her that being a "quality darky" she could hardly be expected to get drunk on whisky "like poor white trash," and that as far as her "free papers" were concerned she would have none of them. There was no use talking, she was

"master's nigger," and he would have to support
her as long as she lived. There was no recourse
but to submit, and the maid continued to follow
her own sweet will until her freedom was forced
upon her by the war. This was no singular or
isolated case.

64865110R00059

Made in the USA
Charleston, SC
15 December 2016